Sports Are the Best!

BASKETBALL IS THE BEST!

by Joe Tischler

PEBBLE
a capstone imprint

Pebble is published by Capstone,
1710 Roe Crest Drive, North Mankato, Minnesota 56003
capstonepub.com

Library of Congress Cataloging-in-Publication Data is available on the Library of Congress website.

ISBN: 9798875256158 (hardcover)
ISBN: 9798875256103 (paperback)
ISBN: 9798875256110 (ebook pdf)

Summary: Easy-to-read text and bright photographs describe the rules, positions, skills, stars, and more of basketball. A short quiz at the end of the book lets the reader test what they've learned.

Editorial Credits
Editor: Erika L. Shores; Designer: Hilary Wacholz; Media Researcher: Rebekah Hubstenberger; Production Specialist: Tori Abraham

Image Credits
Dreamstime: © Aspenphoto, 26; Getty Images: Alika Jenner, 15, Andy Lyons, 23, Candice Ward, 21, Chris Coduto, 14, Christian Petersen, 27, Cooper Neill, 5, Elsa, 6, 17, Ethan Miller, 22, Harry How, 16, iStock/InnaVlasova, 29, Jason Miller, 7, Kanok Sulaiman, 11, real444, cover (right), Tim Nwachukwu, 19; Newscom: Erica Denhoff/Cal Sport Media, 9; Shutterstock: 963 Creation, 24, ARENA Creative, cover (left), BetterPhoto, 13, halwani wani (net), throughout, Lopolo, 10, New Africa (basketball), back cover, 1, 2, 30, PeopleImages.com - Yuri A, 12, Sergey Ryzhov, cover (middle), Tanya Kalian, 25

Printed and bound in China. 006459

Table of Contents

Words in **bold** are in the glossary.

Playing Hoops

Swish! The basketball goes through the net. Sneakers squeak on the shiny court. Players leap to grab a **rebound**. You are at a basketball game!

Basketball started in the United States in 1891. Today, people play it around the world. Men's and women's leagues compete on every continent, except Antarctica. What is it that makes basketball so popular?

CHESAPEAKE ENERGY ARENA
THIS BUD'S FOR YOU.
THUNDER
CHESAPEAKE ENERGY ARENA
HOMELAND
WATCH

Basketball is exciting to watch. On TV, watching replays of high-flying **dunks** is fun. You get to see your favorite players in action.

It is great to attend games in person too. Many basketball **arenas** have activities for kids before or during games. Can you dunk like a pro? There are special courts to test your skills.

The National Basketball Association (NBA) and the Women's National Basketball Association (WNBA) have fun players to watch. NBA star Steph Curry scores from anywhere on the court. WNBA star Caitlin Clark is great at making "logo" three-pointers. She shoots from the logo at midcourt.

Caitlin Clark

What Do You Need to Play Basketball?

Basketball can be both a team and individual sport. It can be played with five teammates, three teammates, or even just by yourself. One-on-one games are good to practice your skills.

Basketball is played indoors or outdoors. Indoor courts are made of wood. Outdoor courts are paved areas in parks, driveways, or schools. Basketball hoops are at each end of the court.

You don't need a lot of equipment to play basketball. You just need a hoop and a ball. You'll want sneakers you can run and jump in.

Basketballs come in different sizes. Younger players use smaller balls. They will also want to find a hoop that can be lowered.

Rules of Basketball

Basketball is an easy game to understand. A player tries to score points in the other team's basket. The team trying to score is called the offense. The team trying to stop the scoring is called the defense.

A player shoots a free throw.

A basketball court has a three-point line. Baskets made behind the line are worth three points. All baskets made on the line or inside the line are worth two points. If a player commits a **foul,** the other team sometimes gets to take a **free throw**. It is worth one point.

Basketball games are divided into two halves. Each half can be 10 to 20 minutes long. Some leagues divide the halves into quarters. The time between halves is called halftime. Players get a break for several minutes.

NBA games have four 12-minute quarters. WNBA games have four 10-minute quarters. Games do not end in ties. If no team is leading when time runs out, the game goes to overtime. In college and professional basketball, they play an extra five minutes.

WNBA teams New York Liberty (in black) and Minnesota Lynx (in white)

Basketball Positions

In a regular game, each team has five players on the court at a time. The players work together to score points for their team.

The offense will try to **dribble** around the defense to get closer to the basket. Players can pass the ball to an open teammate too. Guards, forwards, and centers are the positions players have on the court.

FIRST SECOND ROUNDS
DUQUESNE UNIVERSITY
OAKLAND
4
23
12

Guards play in the **backcourt**. They play farther from the basket. A point guard normally brings the ball up the court. They call out which plays to run. A shooting guard is usually the best scorer on the team.

DUCKS
3
B1G
GM GRAND

Centers and forwards play in the **frontcourt**. They play closer to the basket. Centers grab rebounds and block shots.

Center A'ja Wilson (left) blocks a shot by Courtney Vandersloot.

Power forward Giannis Antetokounmpo grabs a rebound.

Forwards are good at shooting and grabbing rebounds. There are two kinds of forwards—small and power. Small forwards play against both smaller and taller players. Power forwards are better at grabbing rebounds.

Basketball Skills

In basketball, a player has many ways to help their team. Players can work on five important skills. They are dribbling, shooting, running, passing, and jumping.

Dribbling is used to bring the ball up the court. If you stop dribbling, you must either pass or shoot the ball. To score points, you need to be a good shooter. The different types of shots include layups, jump shots, and three-point shots.

A player passes the ball to a teammate.

Basketball players play both offense and defense. That involves a lot of running up and down the court. Passing gets your teammates involved in the offense. A pass that leads to a basket is called an assist.

Jumping is another skill that can show how good a player is. The players who can jump higher are good at grabbing rebounds and blocking shots.

Is Basketball the Best?

Basketball is a sport you can play all year round. You can enjoy it with family and friends. You can also just shoot baskets by yourself. You can challenge yourself. How many free throws can you make in a row?

What's your favorite thing about basketball?

Test Your Basketball Knowledge

Now that you've read this book, are you a basketball expert? Take this quiz to find out! If you don't know the answer, read the book again and you might be able to find it.

1. In a regular game, how many players are on the court for each team?

   a. 3

   b. 4

   c. 5

2. What is one type of forward?

   a. Power

   b. Strong

   c. Short

3. How many points is a free throw worth?

   a. 1

   b. 2

   c. 3

Answers: 1c; 2a; 3a

Glossary

arena (uh-REE-nuh)—a large building with seats for spectators, where sports games and entertainment events are held

backcourt (BAK-kort)—the part of the basketball court that is further away from the basket; guards are considered backcourt players

dribble (DRI-buhl)—to bounce a basketball with your hand

dunk (DUNK)—a type of shot that is thrown down through the hoop

foul (FOWL)—a punishment for breaking a rule in the game

free throw (FREE THRO)—a shot worth one point made from behind the free throw line that is given because of a foul by an opponent

frontcourt (FRUNT-kort)— the part of the basketball court that is closest to the basket; centers and forwards are considered frontcourt players

rebound (REE-bound)—a ball that bounces off the basket after a missed shot; a player who catches ball is given a rebound

Index

About the Author

Joe Tischler is an author and sportswriter who lives in southern Minnesota. When he's not writing about sports, he's watching sports. As a lifelong Minnesotan, he is an avid fan of Minnesota sports teams including the Vikings, Twins, Timberwolves, and Golden Gophers. He's happily married to Gwen and is a proud father to son Toby.